17 71

8/2/95

THE ATMOSPHERE

Design	David West
	Children's Book Design
Editor	Michael Flaherty
Designer	Keith Newell
Picture Researcher	Emma Krikler
Illustrator	Ron Hayward
Consultant	David Flint

© Aladdin Books Ltd 1992

First published in
the United States in 1992 by
Gloucester Press
95 Madison Avenue
New York, NY 10016

Library of Congress Cataloging-in-Publication Data

Clark, John Owen Edward.
    The atmosphere : projects with geography / by John O.E. Clark.
        p.   cm. — (Hands on science)
    Includes index.
    Summary: Discusses Earth's atmosphere and some of the problems
that humans have helped cause, such as acid rain and the
greenhouse effect. Includes related projects.
    ISBN 0-531-17367-4
    1. Atmosphere—Juvenile literature. 2. Atmosphere—Experiments—
Juvenile literature. 3. Human ecology—Juvenile literature. 4. Human
ecology—Experiments—Juvenile literature.
[1. Atmosphere. 2. Atmosphere—Experiments. 3. Man—Infiuence on
nature. 4. Experiments.] I. Title. II. Series.
QC863.5.C53   1992
551.5′078—dc20   92-1514   CIP   AC

Printed in Belgium

HANDS · ON · SCIENCE

THE ATMOSPHERE

JOHN CLARK

GLOUCESTER PRESS
New York · London · Toronto · Sydney

CONTENTS

This book concerns itself with the atmosphere. The topics covered range from the genesis and structure of the atmosphere to the effects the atmosphere has on the earth. The book tells you what causes such phenomena as weather and climate, how they affect the planet and how humankind is altering the atmosphere today. There are "hands on" projects for you to do which use everyday items as equipment. There are also "did you know?" panels of information for added interest.

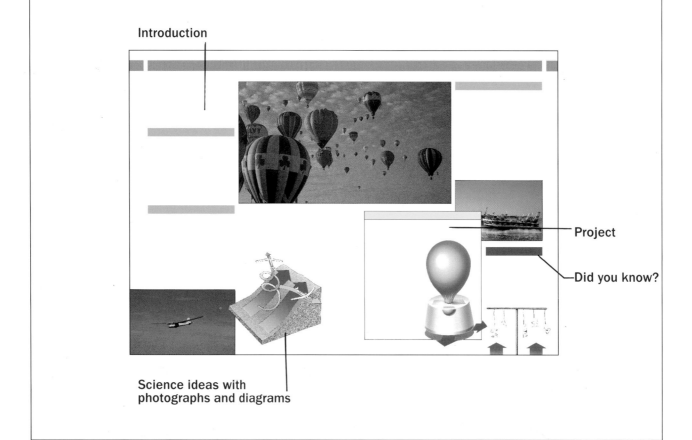

Introduction

Project

Did you know?

Science ideas with photographs and diagrams

INTRODUCTION

The atmosphere is the blanket of air that surrounds the earth, held there by the force of gravity. It consists of a mixture of gases, three of which (nitrogen, oxygen and carbon dioxide) play key roles in the maintenance of life on earth. Movement of the air in the lower atmosphere creates winds, which in turn are responsible for much of our weather.

The atmosphere is not the same all the way up. It is densest near the ground, but gets thinner with altitude until it fades into the nothingness of outer space. Although the atmosphere reaches several hundred miles above our heads, on a global scale proportionally it is as thin as the skin of an apple.

Unfortunately, the activities of humankind are changing the air around us, and atmospheric pollution must be stopped before some of the effects — described in this book — take their toll on life on earth.

Life is dependent on the envelope of air surrounding the earth.

The atmosphere has developed in distinct stages. The early atmosphere was determined by processes involved in the formation of the earth and its early evolution. The development of life has had a great influence on the atmosphere, increasing the oxygen content dramatically over a short period.

first billion years of the earth's life.

As the earth cooled, gases escaped from the interior to form the atmosphere, predominantly through volcanoes. This volcanic activity increased water vapor, carbon dioxide, hydrogen sulfide and nitrogen in the atmosphere.

DEVELOPMENT

The early atmosphere of the earth is believed to have consisted predominantly of nitrogen, carbon dioxide, carbon monoxide, water vapor, hydrogen and inert gases. Solar winds may have removed a lot of the primitive atmosphere in the

Surface cools and early crust forms.

Molten rock and gas form young earth.

Volcanoes release gases and water vapor.

Mountains and sea appear. Plant life evolves.

▷ The proportion of different gases has changed drastically since the evolution of the earth. Nitrogen and oxygen have replaced the hydrogen and carbon dioxide abundant in the early atmosphere.

As water vapor increased, the saturation point of the atmosphere was eventually reached and water started to collect to form the oceans. Carbon dioxide was absorbed into the oceans. Green plants evolved that use sunlight to make carbohydrates from CO_2 and water. Green plants also expel oxygen into the atmosphere. This process is called photosynthesis.

Today's atmosphere appears blue.

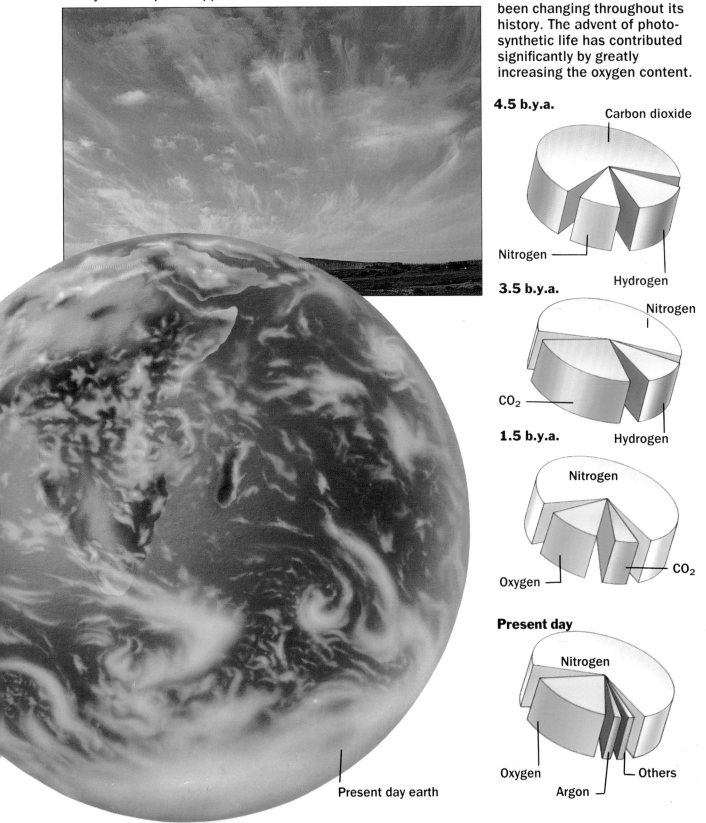

▽ The earth's atmosphere has been changing throughout its history. The advent of photosynthetic life has contributed significantly by greatly increasing the oxygen content.

4.5 b.y.a.

Carbon dioxide

Nitrogen

Hydrogen

3.5 b.y.a.

Nitrogen

CO_2

Hydrogen

1.5 b.y.a.

Nitrogen

Oxygen

CO_2

Present day

Nitrogen

Oxygen

Argon

Others

Present day earth

The atmosphere can be divided into various layers. The bottom layer, the troposphere, extends about 7 miles above the earth's surface. It contains about 80 percent of atmospheric gases. Climatic variations occur in this layer.

Above this the stratosphere extends to 30 miles above the ground and includes the ozone layer which protects the surface from harmful ultraviolet radiation from the sun.

Then the mesosphere extends to about 50 miles above the surface. The temperature drops gradually to a minimum of −300°F.

Above this lies the thermosphere, where temperatures may rise to several thousand degrees Fahrenheit. It stretches over thousands of miles, gradually merging with space. The layer above 300 miles is also called the exosphere.

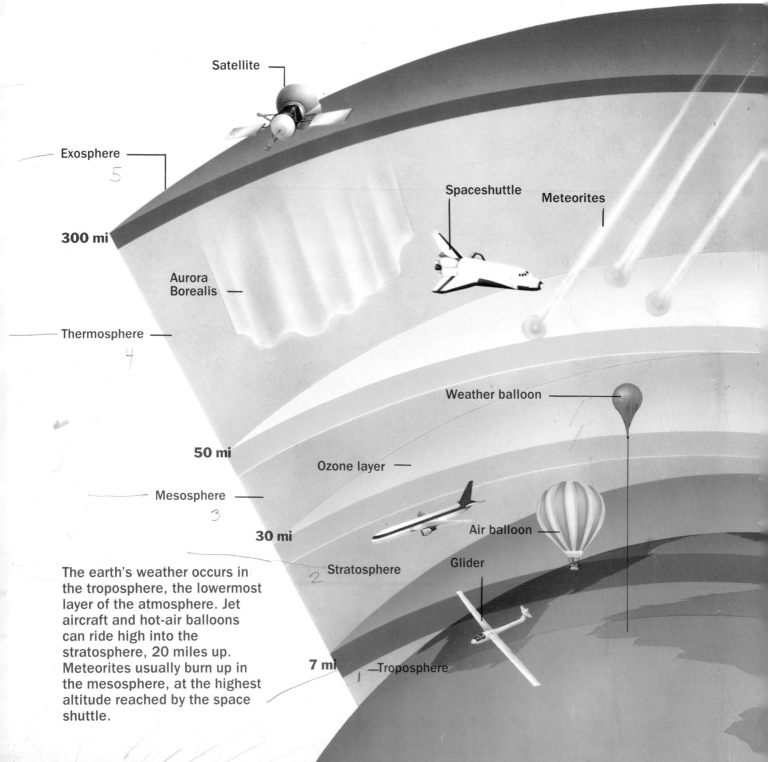

Satellite

Exosphere
5

300 mi

Spaceshuttle   Meteorites

Aurora
Borealis

Thermosphere
4

Weather balloon

50 mi

Ozone layer

Mesosphere
3

30 mi

Air balloon

Glider

Stratosphere
2

The earth's weather occurs in the troposphere, the lowermost layer of the atmosphere. Jet aircraft and hot-air balloons can ride high into the stratosphere, 20 miles up. Meteorites usually burn up in the mesosphere, at the highest altitude reached by the space shuttle.

7 mi   Troposphere

IONOSPHERE

The ionosphere is a layer of electrically charged particles (also called D, E and F layers) between the mesosphere and thermosphere. The particles are ions, which are gas atoms stripped of their electrons. Normally radio waves can only reach places within line-of-sight of the transmitter. But if the waves travel up into the atmosphere, they bounce off the ionosphere and reach distant places.

▷ Long-distance radio communication is possible because radio waves bounce off the ionosphere. The ionized gases in the ionosphere also emit a faint light called an airglow, which prevents even the darkest night sky from being truly black.

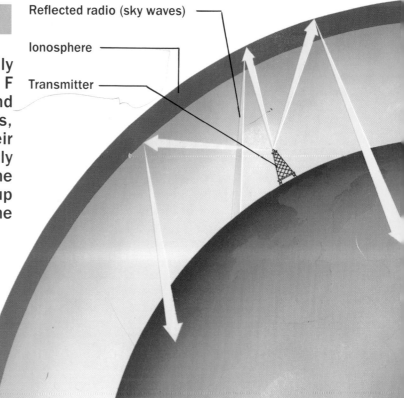

Reflected radio (sky waves)
Ionosphere
Transmitter

△ Solar winds, composed of charged particles streaming out of the sun, collide with the upper atmosphere over the poles resulting in colorful light displays called aurorae.

▷ The red sky of a sunset is caused by dust particles in the atmosphere scattering red light. For this to happen, the air has to be dry indicating that the following day may be fine.

COLORED SKIES

On a cloudless day, the sky looks blue. But the gases in the atmosphere are not colored. White light from the sun is actually made up of all the colors of the rainbow, which when mixed together make white. The gases and dust particles in the atmosphere scatter the blue colors, or wavelengths, of sunlight, more than the other colors so the sky appears to be blue. At sunset, dust near the horizon also scatters the light, but this time it is red that is scattered.

The gases that make up the atmosphere, although light, do have mass. Under the influence of gravity, such as that exerted by the earth, the gases of the atmosphere have weight. But because the atmosphere gets thinner with altitude, most of its mass is concentrated in the thin, lowermost layer, the troposphere.

▷ The 9-mile thick troposphere, the lowermost layer of the atmosphere, contains more than four-fifths of the atmosphere's mass. But because the atmosphere thins with altitude, the troposphere contains only 1.5 percent of the atmosphere's volume.

▽ Mountaineers on high peaks need oxygen masks.

Volume
(a) Mesosphere 93%
(b) Stratosphere 5.5%
(c) Troposphere 1.5%

Mass
(a) Mesosphere 1%
(b) Stratosphere 19%
(c) Troposphere 80%

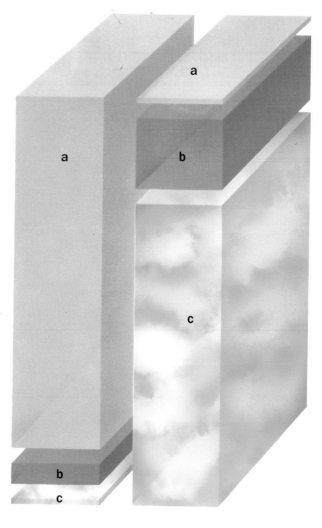

ALTITUDE

The atmosphere gets less dense with altitude — the higher you go, the thinner the air becomes. As the air gets thinner, it contains less oxygen. This has two important consequences. First, high-flying passenger aircraft have to have sealed cabins containing air under pressure so that people can breathe normally. Second, by about 30 miles there is not enough oxygen to burn the fuel in an aircraft's jet engines. Above that height rocket motors have to be used. These burn fuel in the absence of an external source of oxygen.

Altimeters used in aircraft measure height above sea-level. They work in the same way as barometers in measuring changes in atmospheric pressure. Pressure changes can be read from the altimeter and translated accurately into height above sea-level on a dial. The altimeter contains a near-vacuum capsule which alters in size with changes in pressure. This capsule is attached to an arm which relays these movements to a rocking bar, which is in turn attached to a needle on a dial mounted on a hairspring. The dial is calibrated so that pressure changes correspond to height. This enables the pilot to keep the aircraft at the prescribed altitude.

LIGHTER THAN AIR

Because air has density, anything that is less dense than air floats in it — just as a piece of wood, which is less dense than water, floats. Some gases, such as hydrogen and helium, are less dense than air. So a balloon or blimp filled with one of these gases floats in air. Hydrogen is the lightest of all gases, but it is also very flammable and therefore dangerous to use. Helium does not burn and so is generally used for filling weather balloons and blimps. A gas expands and becomes less dense when it is heated. For this reason, it is possible to make a balloon by filling a cloth bag with hot air. Hot-air balloons are used for sport and leisure (see page 20).

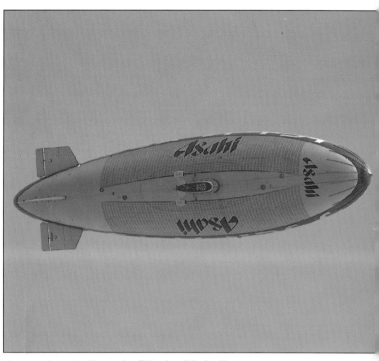

A weather balloon is filled with helium.

WEIGHING AIR

Air has mass and so it can be weighed. To show this, make a sensitive balance. Tie two canes about 20 inches long to a length of string suspended as shown. Attach two balloons to the ends of the lower cane with thread and adjust them until they balance. Mark where the right-hand balloon is and then blow it up with air. Tie it and put it back in the same place. The filled balloon is heavier than the empty balloon because of the air it contains.

DID YOU KNOW?

The density of a substance is its mass divided by its volume. The density of air is about 1.4 ounces per cubic foot. The air in a small bedroom with a volume of 706 cubic feet weighs 62 pounds, or about the same weight as a seven-year-old child.

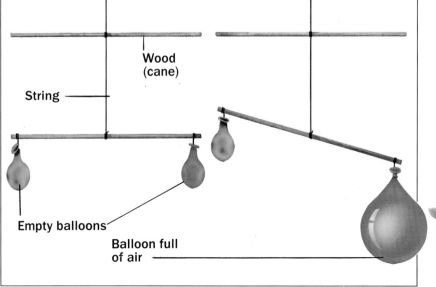

Wood (cane)

String

Empty balloons

Balloon full of air

Air in 1 bedroom

7-yr old child

The mass of air in the atmosphere presses down on the surface of the earth and everything on it. At sea-level, this atmospheric pressure is 14.7 pounds per square foot. But at high altitudes, where the air is much thinner, the pressure decreases, until at the outer edge of the atmosphere it falls to zero.

▽ The air is less dense in the upper atmosphere because there are fewer gas atoms in each cubic foot. The air is therefore at a lower pressure than it is nearer the ground.

Air pressure is lower on high peaks.

Thin air — less gas atoms

Dense air

DISCOVER AIR PRESSURE

Put a sheet of paper over one end of a slim ruler. Hit the other end of the ruler as it hangs over a table. The force preventing the ruler from tipping is air pressure.

WEIGHT OF AIR

The existence of the weight of the air pressing down on everything around us is demonstrated by the simple experiment shown on the left. This natural air pressure also presses on us, and it can be useful. For example, it forces air into our lungs so that we can breathe in the oxygen the atmosphere contains. But in order for us to breathe out again, muscles around our rib cage and diaphragm have to work to squeeze the air out of our lungs at an even higher pressure than that of the atmosphere.

BOILING POINT

When a liquid is heated, molecules leap out of the surface to form a gas or vapor. The vapor has a pressure, called the liquid's vapor pressure. When the vapor pressure equals the atmospheric pressure pushing on the surface of the liquid, the liquid boils. But we have seen that atmospheric pressure varies with altitude, being lower at high altitudes. So what happens when you try to boil a liquid at the top of a high mountain? At sea level, water boils at 212°F. But at high altitudes it boils at temperatures as low as 176°F. This is because the atmospheric pressure is lower and it takes less energy for the vapor pressure to reach the atmospheric pressure.

▷ At low altitudes, water boils at 212°F. At high altitudes, as at the top of a tall mountain, water still boils, but at a much lower temperature.

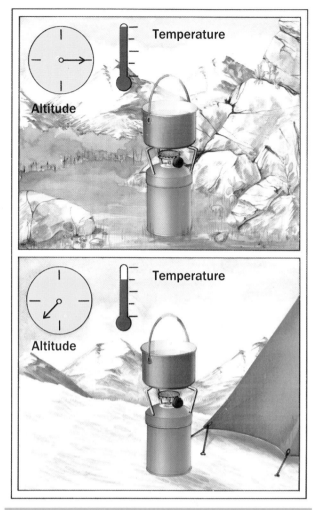

Spacesuits resist the vacuum of space.

AIRLESS SPACE

In outer space, beyond the earth's atmosphere, there is no air at all. Therefore, there is no atmospheric pressure, just an empty vacuum. The vacuum is more complete than any that can be produced in a laboratory. Obviously, a human being cannot breathe in space. Indeed, without atmospheric pressure, a person's blood would boil and his or her body explode. To overcome both of these problems, astronauts who enter free space wear spacesuits. These are pressurized and supplied with air or oxygen, so that the astronaut's lungs can work properly and the boiling point of his body fluids remains normal. The suit also does something else that the atmosphere normally does for us. Its silvery surface reflects back the sun's heat rays and blocks other harmful radiation.

Changes in atmospheric pressure are largely responsible for changes in the weather. The chief effects of pressure changes are winds and other air movements, which in turn control the movements of clouds and rain. For these reasons, weather forecasting relies heavily on measuring air pressure.

HIGH PRESSURE

Cool air sinks to the surface

▽ In high-pressure areas cool air spirals downward — clockwise in the northern hemisphere. In low-pressure areas, warm air spirals upward in the opposite direction.

LOW PRESSURE

Warm air rises

Air is drawn in counterclockwise

Air spirals out clockwise

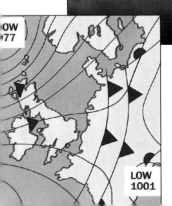

◁ △ Storm clouds often form in areas of low pressure. On a weather map (left), isobars (lines) join places with the same pressure. Isobars close together indicate strong winds.

LOW 1001

HIGHS AND LOWS

When a weather forecaster writes "HIGH" on a weather map, he or she is indicating the location of a high-pressure area in which descending cool air gradually spirals outward. The cone of moving air is called an anticyclone. A "LOW," or low-pressure area, is just the opposite. It occurs when warm air rises, causing it to spiral outward as it climbs. This is called a cyclone or depression.

In the northern hemisphere, the air in an anticyclone spirals in a clockwise direction, whereas a cyclone (depression) has winds rotating counterclockwise. The directions of rotation are reversed in the southern hemisphere. This is due to the effect of the earth's rotation. Anticyclones are usually associated with fine settled weather and light winds near the ground. Cyclones tend to bring cloudy, wet weather with strong winds.

INSIDE A DEPRESSION

In meteorology — the study of weather — the boundary between a mass of warm air and a mass of cold, denser air is called a front. When a mass of cold air forces itself under a mass of warm air, a cold front forms. The warm air is forced up rapidly to create a deep depression, often with heavy rainfall. When a mass of warm air catches up with a mass of cold air, the result is a warm front. The warm air rises only slowly, creating only a shallow depression, and any rain is light or even just drizzle.

▷ On a weather map, the symbol for a cold front is a line with a series of triangles along it. A warm front is represented by a line with a series of semicircles.

MAKING A BAROMETER

Tape plastic wrap over an icecream tub. Attach a pin to one end of a straw, and glue some thread to the other end. Pivot the straw to an upright sheet of cardboard, with a pin stuck into modeling clay. Tape the thread to the plastic wrap, and draw a scale by the pointer.

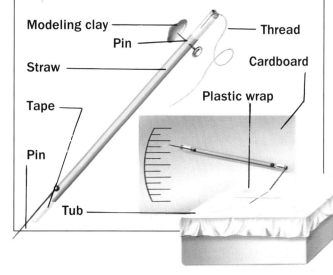

Modeling clay
Pin
Straw
Tape
Pin
Thread
Cardboard
Plastic wrap
Tub

COLD FRONT

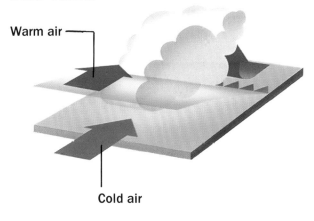

Warm air

Cold air

WARM FRONT

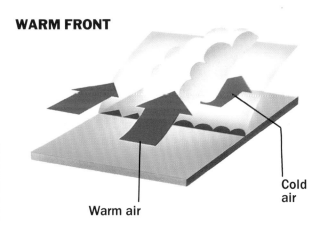

Warm air

Cold air

The barometer on the left works only if the icecream tub is airtight. The outside pressure varies daily, but the pressure in the tub should remain roughly the same. As the outside pressure increases, it pushes in on the plastic wrap causing the pointer to move up the scale. If the outside pressure decreases, the higher pressure in the tub pushes the plastic wrap out causing the pointer to move down across the scale. This works best if the barometer is kept at a constant temperature.

Like all gases, air can be compressed — that is, it can be squeezed so that it occupies a smaller space. But because the smaller volume now contains more gas molecules than usual, the gas exerts a higher pressure. The pressure of a compressed gas can be made to work for us in many ways.

BICYCLE PUMP

The tire on a bicycle contains air at higher than atmospheric pressure. The air is forced into it using a pump, which takes air from the atmosphere and compresses it. The pump consists of a tube or barrel with a tight-fitting piston at the end of a long handle. The piston has a one-way valve that opens to let air into the pump as the handle is drawn back. But when the handle is pushed forward, the valve closes and the piston compresses the air in the tube.

Valve open

Valve closed

On the input stroke of a bicycle pump, the piston is drawn back and air enters the barrel. On the compression stroke, the piston moves forward to compress the air.

PNEUMATIC DRILL

Drills used to dig up the road function through a pneumatic mechanism. The term "pneumatic" means that the drill is driven by compressed air. It is usually driven by a compressor run on a diesel engine. This increases the safety of the drill as it does away with the need for electrical wires trailing across public streets. The drill mechanism causes rapid hammering blows of the drill head on the road surface. This is achieved by a valve in the drill which flips up and down many times a second, rerouting the air around a piston, alternately raising and lowering the drill head.

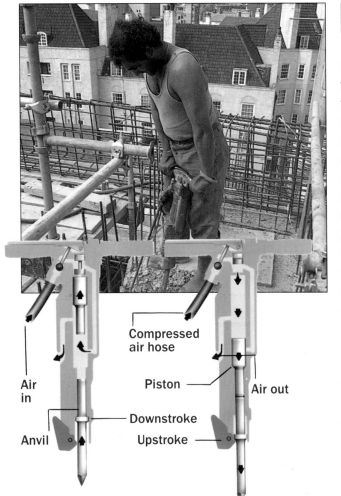

Compressed air hose

Air in

Piston

Air out

Anvil

Downstroke

Upstroke

A pneumatic drill is driven by compressed air, usually from a diesel-engined compressor. The air pressure makes a piston drive the drill point downward.

FIRE EXTINGUISHER

Air is not the only gas that is useful when it is compressed. Carbon dioxide, one of the trace gases in the atmosphere, has many applications. Small cylinders of compressed carbon dioxide are used in domestic carbonated drink-makers. Carbon dioxide gas pressure works various types of fire extinguishers, such as those that spray out a white vapor for putting out electrical fires.

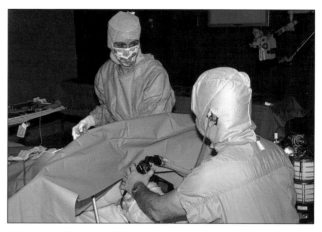
An anesthetist mixes various gases.

A carbon dioxide fire extinguisher

ANESTHETICS

An anesthetist, who is a doctor who puts a patient to sleep for surgery, uses various chemicals, all of which are supplied as compressed gases in metal cylinders. Dentists also sometimes use anesthetic gases. Chief of these are nitrous oxide, once called laughing gas, and a gas called halothane. Anesthetists usually mix these gases with oxygen, also from cylinders.

AEROSOLS

Aerosols are the familiar spray cans that we use every day. They give sprays of a wide range of liquids, from paint and insect killer to perfume and deodorant. The liquid is sold in a metal can, which also contains a propellant gas under pressure. When the button is pressed, it opens a valve so that the compressed gas pushes the liquid up the narrow tube through a jet in the form of a fine spray.

▷ Various gases have been used as propellants in aerosol sprays. Some of the gases used, called CFCs, get into the atmosphere where they damage the ozone layer.

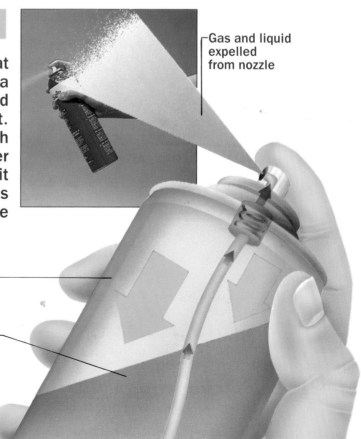
Gas and liquid expelled from nozzle

Gas

Liquid

The key to natural movements of air in the atmosphere is the fact that warm air rises. When it does so, cold air rushes in to take its place. As the warm air cools, it sinks again. This can give rise to a circular flow of air called a wind cell. Such cells give rise in turn to wind currents near the ground.

WIND CELLS

A wind cell is a large, circular, up and down movement of air. There are five massive bands of wind cells girdling the earth: two around each of the polar regions, two around the northern and southern temperate regions, and one around the equator. The air of the temperate cells circulates in the opposite direction to that in the other three bands. They are associated with typical patterns of winds near the earth's surface: the polar easterlies, temperate westerlies and the trade winds near the equator.

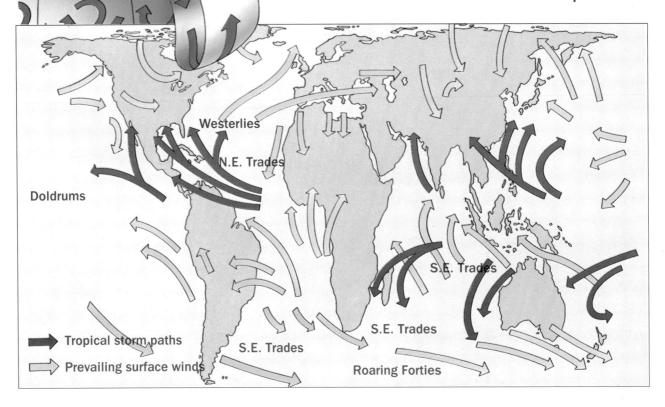

Polar cell
Temperate cell
Tropical cell

Westerlies
N.E. Trades
Doldrums
S.E. Trades
S.E. Trades
S.E. Trades
Roaring Forties

→ Tropical storm paths
⇨ Prevailing surface winds

RELIABLE WINDS

The trade winds follow slightly curved paths toward the equator from the edges of the temperate regions at latitudes 30 degrees north and south. North of the equator, the trade winds blow from the north-east; south of the equator they are south-easterlies. They get their name from an old English word "trade" meaning "track" because they can be relied on always to blow in the same direction, or along the same track.

The basic cause of the trade winds is the upward movement of hot air over the equator. About 2,000 miles north and south, colder air descends. Winds blow from the high pressure areas (cold air) to the low pressure ones (warm air). Similar patterns are repeated farther north and south, so that in most parts of the world the wind blows from one direction most of the time.

HURRICANES

Hurricanes begin from tropical storms usually in late summer. Due to the earth's rotation the storm winds begin to rotate. A hurricane begins to build up and starts moving. The winds around the center can reach speeds of up to 140 mph. The heaviest rains and strongest winds occur about 15-20 miles from the center. A hurricane can travel at speeds between 10-30 mph. Most of the damage is caused when the hurricane crashes ashore bringing massive waves called a storm surge with it.

A hurricane is sustained by warm moist air. Low air pressure at its center causes air to spiral inward. The storm gets its energy from warm tropical water.

Cold air rushes in

Rain clouds

Low air pressure

TORNADOES

A dark, funnel-shaped cloud of dust and wind swirling at up to 280 miles an hour or more is a tornado. A tornado is the most violent kind of storm, and happens when hot, damp air meets cool, drier air. Cold air rushes in at the center, meets the hot air, and may hurtle upward in a spiral at more than 200 miles an hour, sucking up dust and debris as the tornado destroys everything in its path. Most tornadoes occur over land. Over the sea they may suck up huge amounts of water to form a waterspout.

Wall cloud

Descending air

Dust envelope

◁ Resembling a miniature hurricane, a tornado is much more powerful. Its energy is concentrated into a violently rotating column of air less than two thirds of a mile across.

The fact that warm air rises is responsible for winds and much of our weather (see pages 14-15 and 18-19). The reason it rises is because warm air is less dense than cooler air. Several other things make use of this effect, including hot-air balloons, and birds and aircraft that glide on thermals.

HOT-AIR BALLOONS

The first hot-air balloons were made in France in 1783 by the Montgolfier brothers. The brothers were papermakers and these early balloons were made of paper or silk. Today the balloon is made of a fabric such as nylon. A butane gas burner beneath it pumps hot air into the balloon, and a basket hanging beneath the burner carries people. Modern hot-air balloons have reached heights of more than 22 miles.

THERMALS

Currents of rising warm air are called thermals. They often occur near the edges of cliffs or steep hills. Near cliffs, soaring birds such as gulls and fulmars use the thermals over the sea to gain height on stationary wings. Gliders do the same thing, spiraling slowly upward on the updraft of warm air. Even when a glider loses height, a skilful pilot can usually "find" another thermal and spiral upward again.

A modern glider is made of fiber-glass.

Hot-air ballooning is a popular pastime.

▽ After being winched into the air or towed by a powered aircraft, a glider gains extra height by spiraling upward on a thermal of rising warm air.

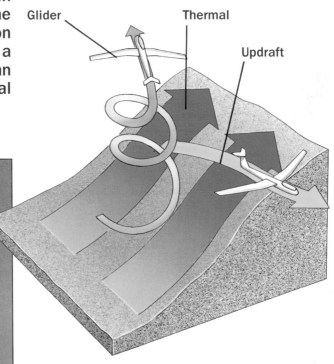

Glider

Thermal

Updraft

AIR CUSHIONS

A different type of air flow can also provide a machine with lift. Air can be forced downward out of the base of a vehicle so that it rides on a cushion of air. This is the principle of the hovercraft, or air-cushion vehicle. It is used mainly for boats and ferries, which often have a flexible rubber skirt around the hull to keep the air cushion in place as the vessel rides over the waves. The air is forced beneath the hull by large fans. Air-cushion vehicles are also used on swampland and even on dry land where there are no real roads.

A passenger-carrying hovercraft

MAKE A HOVERCRAFT

To make a model hovercraft, stick modeling clay on the inside of the bottom of a margarine tub to add weight. Cut a small slit in the middle of the base. Blow up a balloon (not too hard) and, holding the neck tightly, push the neck into the slit. Now watch the model float.

Balloon

Tape

Margarine tub

Modeling clay weight

Air flow

WHAT HAPPENS?

Form a T-shape with two pieces of cane. Hang pieces of foil from the crossbar with thread and place it over a radiator. Warm air rising from the radiator like thermals from the land causes the foil to twist.

Foil

Heat

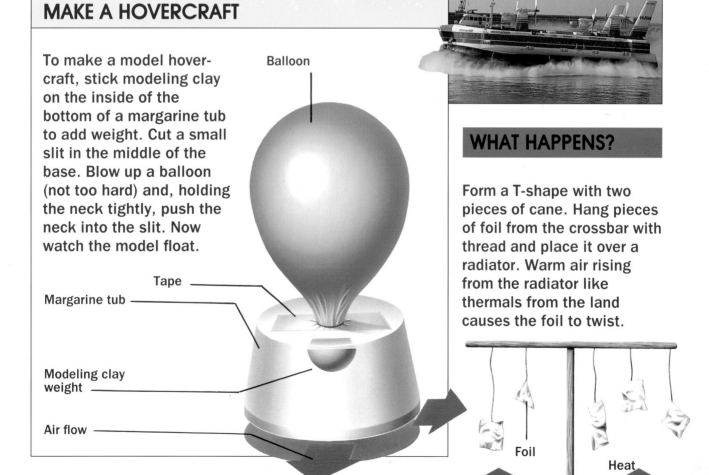

One of the remarkable things about air is its ability to hold moisture in the form of water vapor. Air can hold up to three percent of its volume of water in this way. But a fall in air temperature can precipitate the water as tiny droplets, forming clouds high in the sky, or mist and fog near the ground.

CLOUDS AND RAIN

The sun heats the seas and oceans causing water to evaporate from the surface. It rises on thermals (see page 20) into the air. As this water vapor rises, it may meet cooler air and condense in the form of droplets of water, forming clouds. If the clouds are blown over land and forced to rise over mountains, they get even cooler. The water droplets get bigger and fall as rain. In very cold regions they may freeze and fall as snow. Eventually, rain and melted snow find their way into rivers that carry the water back to the sea. This continual sequence is called the water cycle.

If air near the ground is saturated with water vapor it may cool during the night causing the vapor to condense as fog or form dew.

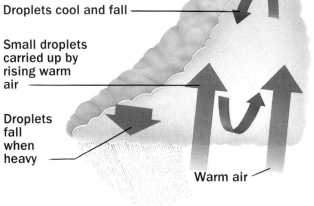

Droplets cool and fall

Small droplets carried up by rising warm air

Droplets fall when heavy

Warm air

▷ The water cycle, sometimes called the hydrological cycle, describes the way in which water vapor from the oceans forms clouds, giving rain which flows back to the sea.

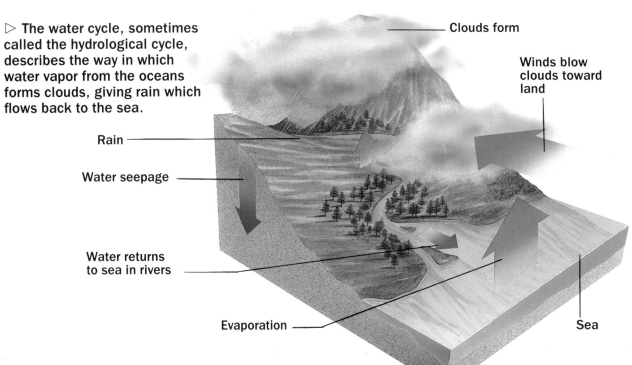

Clouds form

Winds blow clouds toward land

Rain

Water seepage

Water returns to sea in rivers

Evaporation

Sea

RAINBOWS

Invisible water droplets in the air can give rise to one of the most spectacular visible phenomena — a rainbow. It depends on the ability of water — like any other transparent substance — to bend light that passes through it. White sunlight is actually made up of many different colors, or wavelengths (see page 9), and each is bent, or refracted, by a slightly different amount as light enters a raindrop. As long as the drops are at the correct angle to the rays of the sun, we see the separated wavelengths that emerge from the droplets as a rainbow of colors arching across the sky.

△ Rainbows usually appear as low arcs of colors across the sky. If the rainbow is very bright, there may be a second rainbow outside it, with the order of colors reversed.

◁ Light entering a raindrop at the correct angle is split up into its colors. These are reflected from the back of the drop, and split even further as they leave the drop again.

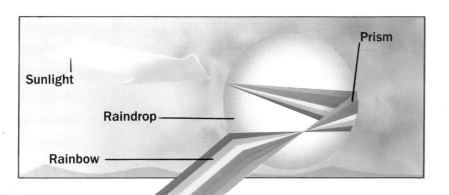

MAKING A RAINBOW

You can make an artificial rainbow, or spectrum, by using water to split sunlight into its component colors. Put some water into a tray or shallow bowl near a window, and angle a mirror so that it reflects bright sunlight coming through the window. Now position a piece of white cardboard near the window to act as a screen to catch the spectrum that is formed.

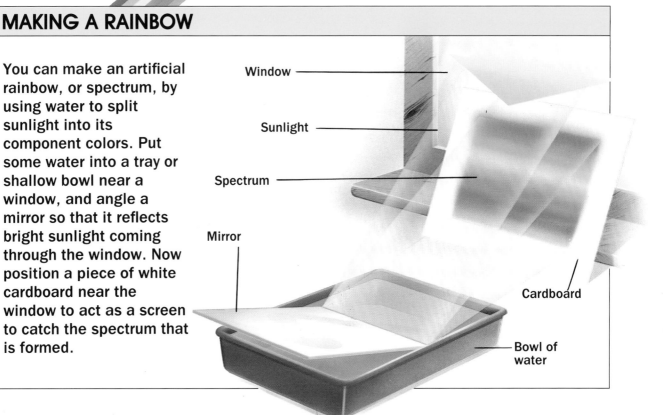

As well as holding water vapor (see page 22), air can also contain particles of dust and smoke, and a whole range of poisonous chemicals. Many forms of atmospheric pollution result from the activities of humankind, such as smoke from factory chimneys and car exhausts, and chemicals from aerosol sprays.

ACID RAIN

When a fossil fuel such as coal or oil is burned, gases such as sulfur oxides and nitrogen oxides are produced. The gases are released into the air in smoke, where they are dispersed by the wind and dissolve in airborne water droplets to form acids. When these droplets finally fall as rain, the acids are released to damage soil and water.

Acid rain can have disastrous effects on the environment. Since the 1960s, acid rain from Britain has been killing fish in lakes in the countries of Scandinavia. In Germany and elsewhere, it has destroyed millions of trees. In towns and cities, acid rain corrodes the stonework of buildings.

△ ▽ Acid rain forms when pollutant gases in the smoke from factories dissolve in water vapor in the air. The rain may fall hundreds of miles away, killing plants and fish.

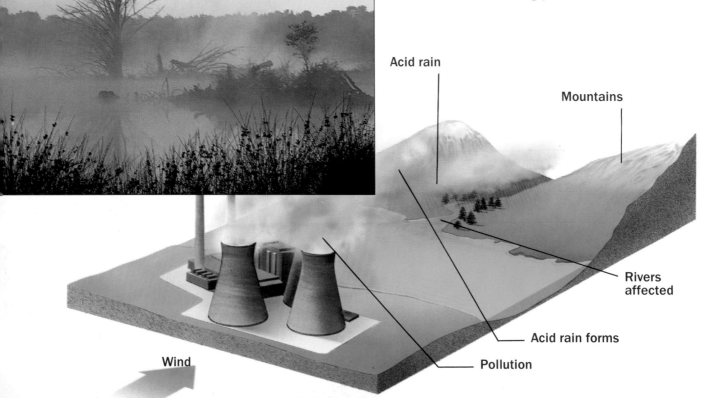

Acid rain

Mountains

Rivers affected

Acid rain forms

Pollution

Wind

SMOG

Fog forms when air saturated with water vapor is cooled below its dew point (see page 22). If the air is over an industrial area, it probably also contains smoke which mixes with the fog to form smog, a choking, acrid mixture that makes people cough. In cities, car exhaust fumes and other pollutants containing hydrocarbons and nitrogen oxides can be converted into photochemical smog by sunlight. Ozone can form in this smog, adding another poison to the air. This smog irritates the eyes and damages lungs. Like acid rain, smog can be prevented by stopping atmospheric pollution.

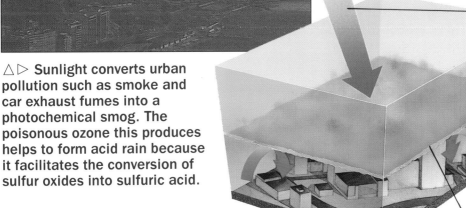

△▷ Sunlight converts urban pollution such as smoke and car exhaust fumes into a photochemical smog. The poisonous ozone this produces helps to form acid rain because it facilitates the conversion of sulfur oxides into sulfuric acid.

Ultraviolet radiation

Trapped heat

City

Smog

THE OZONE LAYER

About 10-20 miles up in the atmosphere is a diffuse layer of the gas ozone. It is a form of oxygen (with three atoms instead of two) and serves to block most of the sun's ultraviolet radiation. This important because too much ultraviolet radiation would be harmful to life on earth. Some substances break up ozone molecules, converting them back to normal oxygen. Among such substances are CFCs, the propellant gases used in some aerosols (see page 17). Satellite photographs have shown a thinning in the ozone layer over the poles, thought to be caused by pollutants like CFCs.

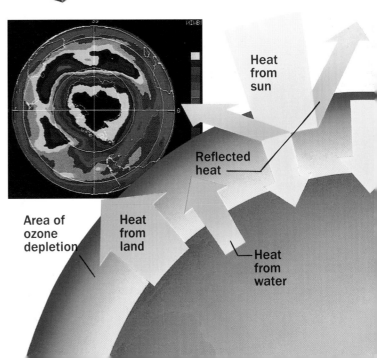

Heat from sun

Reflected heat

Area of ozone depletion

Heat from land

Heat from water

One of the trace gases in the atmosphere is carbon dioxide (it forms only 0.03 percent of air). This gas is an essential part of the carbon cycle. It is released when animals breathe out and organic matter burns or decays, and is the raw material used by green plants in photosynthesis to form carbohydrates.

Burning of trees releases carbon dioxide.

GREENHOUSE GASES

The wholesale burning of the tropical forests releases too much carbon dioxide into the atmosphere. The burning of fossil fuels such as coal and oil has a similar result. Excess carbon dioxide in the atmosphere increases the greenhouse effect. Normally, rays from the sun that reach the surface of the earth warm the ground and are then re-emitted as heat back into space. But carbon dioxide in the atmosphere and the other greenhouse gases (shown below) trap some of the heat. The layer acts like the glass in a greenhouse: it lets warming rays through, but blocks heat trying to get out. One result could be global warming — a gradual increase in temperatures throughout the world. The climate would change dramatically.

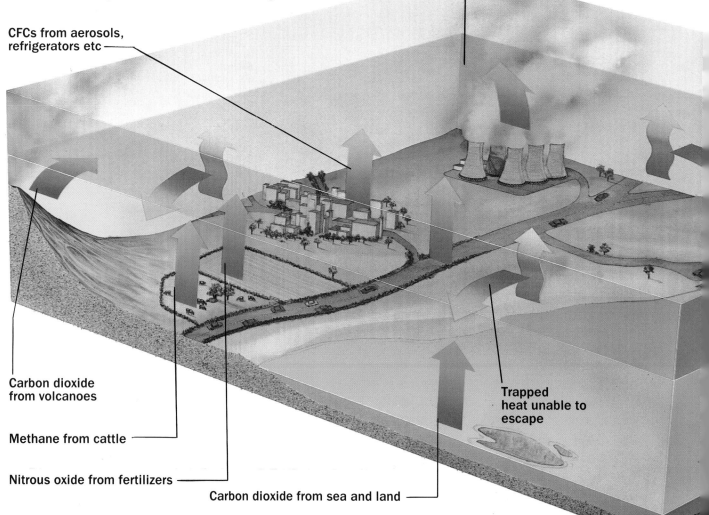

Carbon dioxide from burning of fossil fuels etc

CFCs from aerosols, refrigerators etc

Carbon dioxide from volcanoes

Methane from cattle

Nitrous oxide from fertilizers

Carbon dioxide from sea and land

Trapped heat unable to escape

RISING SEA LEVELS

One possible result of an increasing greenhouse effect is a rise in average temperatures — by as much as two degrees Fahrenheit by the end of the century. As we have just seen, this in turn could start melting the ice of the ice caps at the poles, something that has happened before in the earth's history between the various ice ages. Sea levels would then rise. Many of the world's major cities are built on the coasts. A general rise in sea level of only a few feet would drown many cities near coasts, and some islands in the Pacific would disappear.

△ Erosion of coastlines would increase rapidly if sea levels were to rise. In many places, the sea would encroach on the land, flooding cities and ruining farmland.

▽ Increasing the carbon dioxide content of the atmosphere through pollution and cutting down trees may increase the greenhouse effect to a disastrous degree.

Carbon dioxide in atmosphere

Carbon dioxide from burning wood and deforestation

Carbon dioxide from marine animals

The earth 18,000 years ago

Ice cap over the arctic

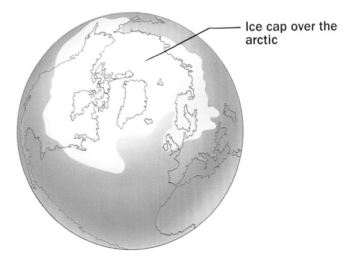

The earth today

Ice cap over the arctic

▷ The average temperature today is only 7° F warmer than the last ice age 18,000 years ago. Due to increasing carbon dioxide levels, the temperature could rise further.

The earth is not alone in having an atmosphere. All the other planets, and even some moons, also have them. But none of them is anything like the atmosphere on earth. None contain oxygen levels required for life like that on earth. And most atmospheres are totally poisonous.

GIANTS AND EARTH'S DOUBLE

The largest planets in the solar system are Jupiter and Saturn. Jupiter's atmosphere consists mainly of the light gases hydrogen and helium, with traces of poisonous ammonia and methane. Violent storms rage in the atmosphere, with winds of up to 200 miles per hour. Saturn's atmosphere is similar, and like Jupiter has bands of counterflowing easterly and westerly winds. Venus is a similar size to earth, and is covered by a dense atmosphere consisting mostly of clouds of carbon dioxide and sulfuric acid.

▽ The mainly carbon dioxide atmosphere of Venus is so dense that, at the surface of the planet, atmospheric pressure is 90 times as high as it is at sea level on earth.

△ The most distinctive feature in Jupiter's atmosphere is a whirlpool of gases known as the great red spot. It has been there for at least 300 years.

▽ The famous ring system of Saturn consists of millions of particles of dust and ice, probably coming originally from the planet's atmosphere.

ATMOSPHERIC MOONS

Earth's moon has no atmosphere at all. But some of the moons of the giant planets have retained an atmosphere. Saturn's largest natural satellite, Titan, is much larger than our moon and has a substantial atmosphere consisting of thick clouds of methane. Io, also slightly larger than our moon, is the closest of Jupiter's large satellites and is dotted with active volcanoes. These throw various gases into its atmosphere, and even coat neighboring Amalthea with sulfur. Scientists wonder if the composition of its atmosphere is similar to that of primitive earth's.

△ Voyager space probes took close-up pictures of Jupiter's moon Io, revealing its active volcanoes with streaks of ash and sulfur.

▷ Titan, the largest moon of Saturn, is the only body in the solar system other than a planet to have a proper atmosphere. It is so thick that it hides Titan's surface.

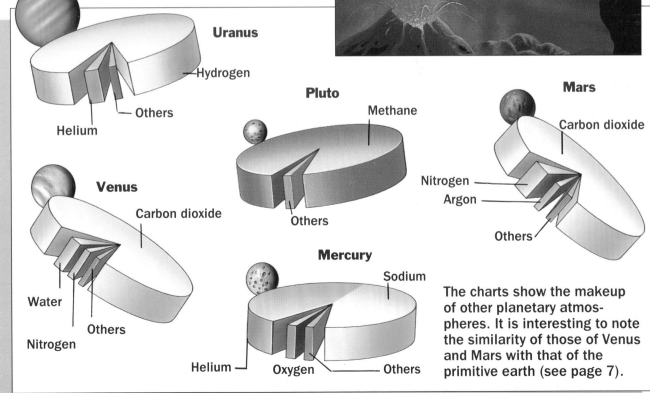

Uranus
— Hydrogen
— Others
Helium

Pluto
Methane
Others

Mars
Carbon dioxide
Nitrogen —
Argon —
Others

Venus
Carbon dioxide
Water
Others
Nitrogen

Mercury
Sodium
Helium —
Oxygen
Others

The charts show the makeup of other planetary atmospheres. It is interesting to note the similarity of those of Venus and Mars with that of the primitive earth (see page 7).

In the total absence of air or any other gas, we are left with a vacuum. Vacuums have their drawbacks — sound will not travel through them. But they also have their uses, some of which are described on this page. But the best vacuums produced on earth are still not as "perfect" as the vacuum of outer space.

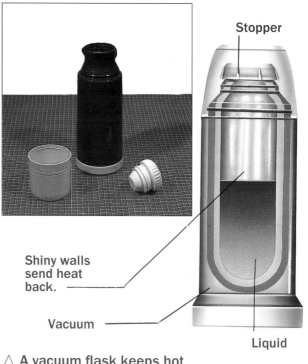

Stopper

Shiny walls send heat back.

Vacuum

Liquid

△ A vacuum flask keeps hot liquids hot, or cold liquids cold, by eliminating all three ways that heat can travel.

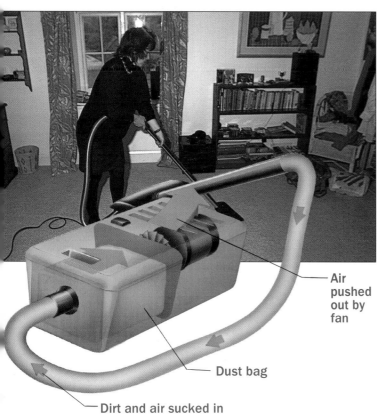

Air pushed out by fan

Dust bag

Dirt and air sucked in

△ A vacuum cleaner uses a motor-driven fan to force air out of the back. Air rushing in brings with it dust and dirt.

The vacuum flask was invented at the end of the last century by the British scientist James Dewar. The vacuum between two thin glass walls prevents heat transmission by conduction (through contact between a hot object and something else) or convection (movement of heat by a liquid or gas). Silvering prevents transmission by radiation.

A vacuum cleaner is better described as a suction cleaner. It does not create a true vacuum, just a low-pressure region which external air rushes into carrying dust and dirt. A removeable collecting bag catches the dust from the air.

In the absence of radio communications, astronauts cannot communicate with each other no matter how loud they shout. The vacuum of space will not carry sound. But if they touch helmets, sound vibrations (and speech) travel from one to the other.

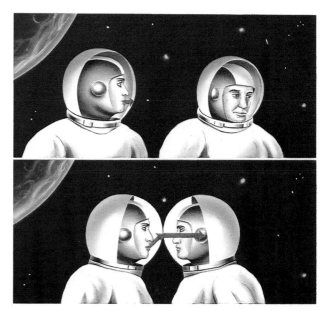

Anticyclone
Region of high pressure in the atmosphere with winds that spiral outward.

CFCs
Organic gases (chlorofluorocarbons) used in refrigerators and aerosol sprays; released into the atmosphere, they can damage the ozone layer.

Convection
Movement of a fluid (gas or liquid) caused by differences of temperature within it. Warm fluid rises; cool fluid descends.

Cyclone
A region of low pressure in the atmosphere with winds that spiral inward.

Density
The mass of a substance divided by its volume.

Depression
An area of low pressure in the atmosphere.

Exosphere
The outermost layer of the atmosphere above an altitude of about 300 miles.

Ionosphere
A layer in the atmosphere, at between 50 and 200 miles above the earth, that contains charged gas atoms (ions); it is important in long-distance radio communications.

Mesosphere
The layer of the atmosphere between 30 and 50 miles above the earth.

Newton
A force that provides a mass of 1 kg with an acceleration of 1 ms^{-2}.

Ozone
A form of oxygen with three atoms in each molecule (instead of the usual two atoms).

Ozone layer
A layer of ozone in the atmosphere at a height of between 10 and 20 miles. It blocks much of the sun's harmful ultra-violet radiation, but may be damaged by atmospheric pollutants such as CFCs.

Pressure
The size of a force divided by the area it acts on.

Smog
A mixture of smoke and fog which sometimes forms in the air over cities and industrial areas.

Spectrum
The colors of the rainbow which, when mixed together, form white light. Each color has a different wavelength.

Stratosphere
The layer of the atmosphere between 10 and 30 miles above the earth.

Thermal
A rising current of warm air.

Thermosphere
The layer of the atmosphere beween 200 and 300 miles above the earth.

Trace gases
Gases found in small amounts, that are essential for all living things.

Troposphere
The lowest layer of the atmosphere, between the earth's surface and an altitude of 10 miles.

Photographic Credits:
Cover and pages 11 and 20 top: Eye Ubiquitous; pages 5, 7, 13, 17 middle, 24 top and 18 top: The J. Allan Cash Photo Library; pages 9 top, 19 top and 28 bottom right: The Science Photo Library; page 9 bottom: Dan Brooks; pages 10, 14 and 25 bottom: Frank Spooner Pictures; pages 12 and 25 top: The Hutchison Library; pages 15, 16 top, 17 top and bottom and 30 top and bottom: Roger Vlitos; page 16 bottom: Paul Nightingale; pages 19 bottom and 26: Robert Harding Picture Library; pages 20 bottom, 21, 22, 23 and 27: Spectrum Color Library; page 24 bottom: Topham Picture Source; pages 28 bottom left and 29 top and bottom: David A Hardy F.B.I.S., L.R.P.S.